★GETTING TO KNOW★
ITALY
and ITALIAN

Written by
Emma Sansone

Illustrated by
Kim Woolley

Watts

LONDON • NEW YORK • SYDNEY

Contents

	Map of Italy	4
	Facts about Italy	6
	Regions of Italy	8
	Rome	10
	In a typical Italian town	12
	Eating in Italy	14
	What people do	16
	Children in Italy	18
	History of Italy	20
	Famous places	22
	Festivals	24
	Speaking Italian	26
	At the café	28
	At the shops	30
	Index	32

Produced by Times Four Publishing Ltd,
5 High Street, Cuckfield, Sussex RH17 5EN

Edited by Nicola Wright
Designed by Chris Leishman
Additional illustration by Guy Smith
Consultant Naomi Laredo

Colour separations by RCS Graphics Ltd, Leeds
Typeset by Typografica, Hove, East Sussex
Printed by Proost, Belgium

First published in 1992 by The Watts Group

Copyright © Times Four Publishing Ltd

BRITISH LIBRARY CATALOGUING IN PUBLICATION DATA
A catalogue record for this book is available from the British Library.

ISBN 0 7496 0901 X HB   ISBN 0 7496 3004 3 PB

10 9 8 7 6 5 4 3 2 1

About this book

In this book you can find out about Italy – its people, landscapes and language. For example, discover what the Italians like to eat and drink, what they do for a living, and what famous Italian places look like.

Where Italy is in the world

Find out, also, what schooldays are like for Italian children, and about their holidays and festivals. On page 26 there is a special section to introduce you to speaking Italian.

Hello!

Ciao!

It explains how to use and pronounce everyday words and phrases, so you can make friends and ask for things in cafés and shops. Also, some Italian words and their meaning are given throughout the book to help you increase your vocabulary.

Map of Italy

Italy is in southern Europe. In the north it has borders with France, Switzerland, Austria and Slovenia. The Mediterranean Sea borders Italy to the east, west and south. The country is easy to recognize on a map, because it is shaped like a high-heeled boot. The island of Sicily is just by the toe of Italy. The island of Sardinia is further out to the north-west.

Highest mountain:
Mont Blanc (Monte Bianco), Alps, 4,807 metres. It is the highest mountain in western Europe and lies along the Italian-French border.

The Italian landscape is very varied. In the north there are high mountains and a large flat plain. Along the east coast there are long beaches. The west coast is more rocky. Mountains and hills run all the way down the middle of the country, like a backbone. Some of these mountains are volcanoes.

Key

★ Capital city

  Major town

  Seaside resort

  Port

▲ Volcano

Longest river:
River Po, 652 km. The river flows from the Alps to the Adriatic Sea. Rice is grown in huge fields along the river valley.

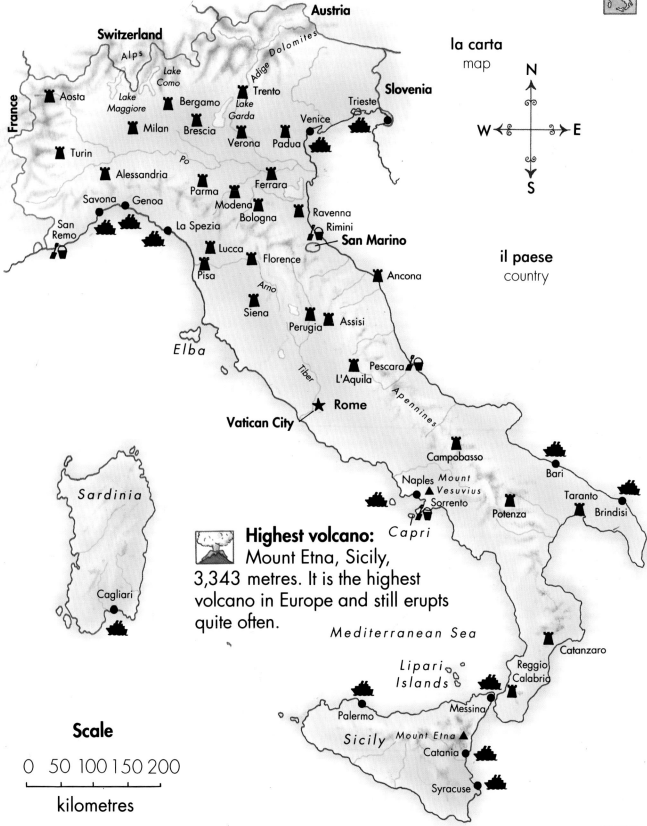

la carta
map

N
W ← → E
S

il paese
country

Switzerland

Austria

Alps

Slovenia

France

Aosta

Lake Como

Lake Maggiore

Trento

Bergamo

Adige

Dolomites

Trieste

Milan

Brescia

Lake Garda

Venice

Turin

Verona

Padua

Po

Alessandria

Parma

Ferrara

Savona

Genoa

Modena

Bologna

Ravenna

San Remo

La Spezia

Rimini

San Marino

Lucca

Florence

Ancona

Pisa

Siena

Arno

Perugia

Assisi

Elba

Tiber

L'Aquila

Pescara

Rome

Apennines

Vatican City

Campobasso

Bari

Naples

Mount Vesuvius

Taranto

Sorrento

Potenza

Brindisi

Capri

Sardinia

Catanzaro

Cagliari

Highest volcano:
Mount Etna, Sicily,
3,343 metres. It is the highest
volcano in Europe and still erupts
quite often.

Mediterranean Sea

Lipari Islands

Reggio Calabria

Palermo

Messina

Sicily

Mount Etna

Scale

0 50 100 150 200

kilometres

Catania

Syracuse

Facts about Italy

Italy is a little bigger than the United Kingdom and has a slightly larger population. There are so many mountains that most people live in cities and towns in the plains and on the coasts.

 Size:
301,225 sq km

la bandiera
flag

 Population:
57,590,000

The Italian flag is green, white and red. It is called the 'tricolore', which means a flag with three colours.

The Head of State is the President, who is elected by Parliament every seven years. But most important decisions about the way the country is run are made by the Prime Minister and the Government.

Capital city:
Roma (Rome)

Official name:
Italia or Repubblica Italiana (Italian Republic)

Language

Although the official language is Italian, other languages are also spoken in parts of the country:

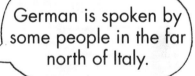

German is spoken by some people in the far north of Italy.

la lingua
language

In most regions of Italy, many people also speak a local variety of their language, called a dialect.

Near the French border in the north-east, some Italians speak French.

Money

Italian money is counted in lire. The smallest coin is ten lire. A packet of chewing gum costs about 100 lire.

There are many different coins and bank notes. Coins are usually made in amounts of 50, 100, 200 and 500 lire. The head of a woman is shown on the coins, representing Italy.

i soldi
money

Bank notes are issued for 1000, 2000, 5000, 10,000, 50,000 and 100,000 lire. The heads of famous Italian people appear on the notes.

Some things made in Italy

la pizza
pizza

l'olio d'oliva
olive oil

il vino
wine
Chianti, Asti Spumante,
Barolo, Soave

la pasta
pasta
spaghetti, macaroni,
vermicelli

la macchina
cars
Ferrari, Fiat,
Lancia

i vestiti
clothes
Benetton,
Gucci, Armani

Regions of Italy

Italy is divided into 20 regions, including the islands of Sicily and Sardinia in the Mediterranean. The scenery, weather and way of life vary greatly from region to region.

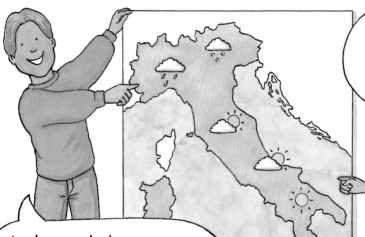

In the south the winter is cool, the spring is sunny and fresh, and the summer is hot and very dry.

il tempo
weather

In the north the winter is very cold, spring and autumn are very wet, and summer is hot and dry.

la neve
snow

In the north, the high mountains of the Alps are covered with snow most of the year. There are many ski resorts for winter holidays, and in summer people go hiking.

There are also some large lakes among the mountains. The beautiful scenery attracts many visitors.

In the mountains there are wildlife parks, where you can find animals such as deer, chamois, mountain goats and lynxes.

il lago
lake

Just south of the Alps is a large plain, the Pianura Padana. It is good farmland where farmers grow wheat, maize and rice.

The western coastline is generally rocky, with many inlets. The eastern coastline is flatter, with long, sandy beaches. There are many holiday resorts along both coasts.

Tuscany, Umbria and Latium, in central Italy, are hilly. The country-side is beautiful, with picturesque towns and villages, and castles.

In the south-east region of Apulia, farmers live in houses with cone-shaped stone roofs.

In the south, people grow tomatoes, oranges and lemons. Grapes are grown almost everywhere.

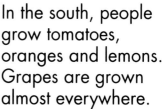

Southern Italy (the 'foot' of the 'boot') is very rocky. Towns have been built on the steep slopes of the mountains.

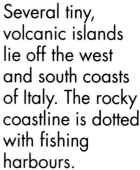

Several tiny, volcanic islands lie off the west and south coasts of Italy. The rocky coastline is dotted with fishing harbours.

Rome

Rome is Italy's capital city. It is also the largest city in Italy. Nearly three million people live there.

It is a very ancient city. Originally it was built on seven hills beside the River Tiber, about 25 km from the sea. The ancient Romans conquered most of Europe, and Rome was the capital of their empire. You can still see some of their ancient monuments, like the Colosseum and the ruins of the Roman Forum.

Now the city has grown so much that the outskirts reach almost to the sea, and traffic problems are terrible.

You can get around Rome by bus, but the fastest way is by Metro, the underground railway.

In the centre, there are many beautiful churches, squares and fountains. There are cafés all around, where people like to sit outside, drink coffee and eat ice-cream.

Famous places

Colosseo
(ancient Roman arena)

Monumento a Vittorio Emanuele
(built to celebrate the unification of Italy)

Pantheon
(a Roman temple to the gods, which later became a Christian church)

Arco di Constantino
(ancient Roman arch built to celebrate Emperor Constantine)

Basilica di San Pietro
(a huge Roman Catholic church in the Vatican City, home of the Pope)

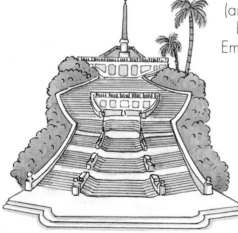

Piazza di Spagna and the Spanish Steps
(a beautiful square with a long staircase and a fountain shaped like a boat)

Fontana di Trevi
(people say that if you throw a coin into this fountain you are sure to return to Rome one day)

In a typical Italian town

Most Italian towns and villages are built around a square. There is usually a church on one side, shops, and at least one bar. When it is sunny, the bar has tables outside.

la gelateria
ice-cream shop

l'edicola/il giornalaio
newsagent's

la tabaccheria
tobacconist's

la chiesa
church

il bar
bar/café

FARMACIA

l'ufficio postale
post office

la farmacia
chemist

la macelleria
butcher's

We generally wear navy blue uniforms in winter, white uniforms in summer, and white helmets.

i vigili urbani
town police

Old people like to sit in the square with their friends and watch what is going on. Young people often meet their friends in the bar.

The church plays an important part in village life. On Sunday mornings, families dress up and go to Mass. Most people in Italy are Roman Catholics.

alimentari/la drogheria
grocer's

la libreria
bookshop

la banca
bank

l'ufficio turistico
tourist office

la cartoleria
stationer's

la pasticceria
cake shop

il supermercato
supermarket

il negozio di abbigliamento
clothes shop

il municipio
town hall

la panetteria
bakery

il negozio di ferramenta
hardware store

Eating in Italy

Italians love their food and enjoy eating out. Each region of Italy has its own special foods.

Italians don't eat much for breakfast. Children normally have a cup of milk and some biscuits or bread and jam. Adults like to put coffee in their milk. Some have a little cup of strong black coffee on its own.

People often have a snack (uno spuntino) half way through the morning. Children eat this at break-time in school.

la colazione
breakfast

il caffè
coffee

il pane
bread

il latte
milk

la marmellata
jam

il burro
butter

Lunch (il pranzo) is usually between 1 pm and 2 pm. People normally start with pasta or rice. The second course is usually meat or fish, with bread and vegetables or a salad. The meal ends with fresh fruit. Desserts are only eaten on Sundays or on special occasions.

Supper (la cena) is in the evening, between 7 pm and 9 pm. The first course can be pasta, rice or soup. Then people normally eat cheese and cold meats, or an omelette, with bread and vegetables. They finish with fresh fruit again.

Some typical Italian dishes:

risotto alla milanese
rice cooked with stock, white wine and saffron

pizza alla napoletana
pizza with mozzarella cheese, tomato, anchovy and oregano

spaghetti alla bolognese
spaghetti with a meat sauce

saltimbocca alla romana
little slices of veal with ham, sage and sweet wine

pesce spada alla griglia
grilled swordfish cutlets

gelato
ice-cream

peperonata
peppers cooked with onions and tomatoes

lasagne
thin layers of pasta with meat sauce, white sauce and cheese

torrone
hard nougat with almonds or hazelnuts

zabaglione
warm creamy dessert made with eggs yolks, sugar and sweet wine

vino
wine
Barolo, Chianti, Soave

aperitivo
aperitif
Martini, Campari

birra
beer
Peroni

granita
lemon or coffee (iced drink)

Drinks

What people do

In Italy, people live and work differently in the various regions. There are large industrial areas where people work in factories. Some people work as farmers in the countryside. Tourism also provides many jobs.

la fabbrica
factory

Industry has grown quickly in Italy. More people now work in industry than in farming. Most of the factories are in the north, around the great cities of Milan, Turin and Genoa.

Many people in Milan work in the fashion and textile industries.

Pottery and leather are made in Tuscany and Umbria. Venice is famous for its beautiful ornamental glass.

Italy also produces ships, cars, chemicals, machinery and electrical goods such as computers.

The tourist industry employs many people, especially along the coasts, by the lakes and in the Alps. They run hotels, restaurants, cafés and bars.

l'uva
grapes

Wine is very important in Italy. There are vineyards in almost every region. Some grapes are grown to be eaten, but most are made into wine. Some Italian wines are very famous, and are sold all over the world.

CHIANTI CLASSICO

Around the coast there are many ports, and fishing is very important. A large number of people work in the fishing industry.

il pescatore
fisherman

l'agricoltore
farmer

Cattle are kept on the plains and in some rich pastures in the Alps. Further south, in the Apennine mountains, farmers keep sheep. Pecorino and ricotta cheeses are made from sheep's milk.

le pecore
sheep

le mucche
cows

Olives are grown all over Italy except in the far north. They are used for making olive oil, and for eating.

l'oliva
olive

Peaches, nectarines, apricots, plums, oranges, lemons and tomatoes are grown all along the west and east coasts. Many are exported to the rest of Europe.

17

Children in Italy

Here you can find out something about school life in Italy, and about how Italian children spend their time.

la scuola
school

The school day usually begins at 8.30 in the morning, and ends around 1 o'clock. Then children go home for lunch. There is no school in the afternoon, but there is homework to do every day. Many children also have to go to school on Saturdays.

Italian children have no half-term holiday, but their summer holiday is longer than in Britain.

i compiti
homework

We have two weeks' holiday at Christmas, two weeks at Easter, and nearly three months in the summer.

Most Italian families take their holidays in Italy. In the summer they may go to the seaside or to the mountains to get away from the heat.

le vacanze
holidays

Because the summer holidays are so long, most children have to do 'i compiti delle vacanze' (holiday homework) to revise what they learned at school during the year.

i ragazzi
children

In most Italian schools, pupils do not wear a uniform. In primary schools children wear blue or black overalls on top of their clothes, so they won't get too dirty.

Older children like to wear jeans and sweatshirts and fashionable trainers.

There is not much time for sports in Italian schools. Children who like sports generally practise them in the afternoons. Football is the most popular sport with boys. Many girls like volley ball and basketball. Swimming and tennis are popular in the summer.

Schools in the north of Italy often take their pupils on a 'settimana bianca' (white week) in January or February. The whole class spends a week in a ski resort. They have some lessons, but spend most of the time skiing, tobogganing and practising winter sports.

Italian children enjoy reading comics. Walt Disney characters are the favourites, but Garfield, Charlie Brown and Asterix are also very popular.

Computer games are also popular.

History of Italy

Rome was founded in 753 BC. The Romans went on to conquer most of Europe, and Italy became the centre of their vast empire.

In the 5th century AD, barbarians such as the Huns, Goths and Vandals from Northern Europe invaded Italy, and the Roman Empire fell.

For many centuries after the fall of the Roman Empire, Italy was divided into small states. The French, Spanish, Arabs and Austrians all tried to conquer Italy for themselves.

In the 19th century, the people rebelled against foreign occupation. The people's hero, Giuseppe Garibaldi, successfully led the fight in 1860.

In 1870, Italy was united into one independent country, with Rome as its capital. Victor Emmanuel II was proclaimed King of Italy.

During World War I Italy fought on the side of Britain and France. After the war, Benito Mussolini became dictator in 1922. Under his rule, in 1940, Italy entered World War II on the side of Germany.

1922

After World War II, Italy became a republic. In 1958 Italy joined France, West Germany, Belgium, Luxembourg and the Netherlands to form the European Economic Community.

1958

Famous Italians

Marco Polo (1254–1324) Explorer who travelled from Europe to Asia.

Christopher Columbus (1451–1506) Explorer who reached the West Indies and America.

Leonardo da Vinci (1452–1519) Artist who painted the most famous painting in the world, the Mona Lisa, now in the Louvre in Paris.

Michelangelo Buonarroti (1475–1564) Artist who sculpted the famous statue of David, now in Florence.

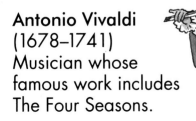

Antonio Vivaldi (1678–1741) Musician whose famous work includes The Four Seasons.

Galileo Galilei (1564–1642) Scientist who invented the pendulum and the astronomical telescope.

Famous places

Every year, millions of tourists come to Italy from all over the world. The country has many art treasures and historic remains as well as beautiful countryside. These are some of the places they come to see.

Courmayeur is a famous ski resort near Mont Blanc. It has a French name because it is so close to the French border.

il canale
canal

Venice is a unique city, built on hundreds of tiny islands, with canals for streets and boats for buses. St Mark's Square is the largest and most famous in Venice.

The Ponte Vecchio crosses the river Arno in Florence. It is lined with workshops and houses.

Florence is a beautiful city, full of masterpieces of painting and sculpture, as well as famous buildings.

Capri is a small island off the coast of Naples where the Roman emperor Tiberius built several villas. Tourists like to admire the views and, of course, sunbathe and swim.

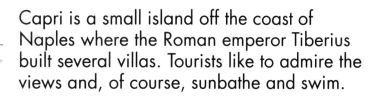

Pompeii was an ancient Roman town near Naples. It was buried by lava and ash from Mount Vesuvius in AD 79. Today you can visit the ruins, and see houses, streets, shops, even Latin graffiti on the walls.

la torre
tower

Parts of the rocky coast of Sicily are covered in orange trees and plants called oleanders. Visitors can also see ancient Greek remains.

The Leaning Tower of Pisa is one of the most famous sights in Italy. The tower leans so much that tourists are no longer allowed to climb up the spiral staircase inside.

There are boat trips around Lake Maggiore. The palace on the tiny island of Isola Bella was built for Isabella, the wife of Count Carlo Borromeo.

l'isola
island

Festivals

Italians love celebrations. There are many festivals in the year. Some take place all over Italy, and some are held just in certain regions. Many villages have their own special feast days.

The week before Ash Wednesday is Carnival time. All over Italy people wear fancy dress, and there are lots of funfairs and parades with floats. The Carnival in Venice is spectacular, with gorgeous costumes and processions of gondolas.

il carnevale
carnival

la gara
race

il cavallo
horse

On 2 July and on 15 August, a horse race called the Palio is run in Siena. People from the different quarters of the town dress up in medieval costume, and there are processions to the main square. Here, riders from each quarter compete in the race. The prize is an embroidered banner.

In summer, in towns and villages all over Italy, people have fairs sponsored by different political parties.

There are picnics and barbecues, food stalls, open-air discos, bands, singers and pop concerts.

24

la statua
statue

Most towns and villages celebrate the feast of their patron saint with a procession. A statue of the saint is carried through the streets and people follow with candles and flowers.

In the wine-producing areas, people celebrate the end of the grape harvest in the autumn. They hold fairs and dances, and taste the new wine. Often special foods from the region are sold in the markets.

On 7 December, in Milan, the feast of the city's patron saint, St Ambrose, is celebrated with a market fair around his church. There are stalls selling doughnuts, candy floss and special sausages, as well as gifts.

On 6 January, La Befana (an old ragged woman who rides a broomstick) brings sweets to children in Rome. But if they have been naughty she leaves them a piece of coal instead.

i fuochi d'artificio
fireworks

At New Year, people in Naples let off fireworks and throw old crockery out of the windows, to show they are making a new start. All the ships in the harbour hoot, and there are huge firework displays.

Speaking Italian

You will find some useful Italian words on the following pages, plus some simple phrases to help you to ask for things.

Every word is written in three different ways:

these are the Italian words

un succo d'arancia
(oon soocko d'arancha)
orange juice

this gives you an idea of how to pronounce the Italian

this is what it means in English

In each speech bubble you will find an Italian phrase, a guide to pronouncing it and its English meaning. You will see how easy it is to go shopping or to order what you want to eat and drink at a café.

the Italian words

how to pronounce the Italian words

the English translation

Vorrei un gelato
(Vorray oon jelarto)
I would like an ice-cream

Making friends

Here are some simple Italian phrases to use when you want to make friends.

Sì
(See)
Yes

Per favore
(Pair favoray)
Please

Ciao
(Chow)
Hello

Buongiorno
(Bwon jorno)
Good morning

Scusami
(Skoozamee)
Excuse me

Signore
(Seenyoray)
Mr, Sir

Parli inglese?
(Parlee eenglayzay?)
Do you speak English?

Ciao. Come ti chiami?
(Chow. Komay tee kee-armee?)
Hello. What is your name?

Mi chiamo Maria. E tu?
(Mee kee-armo Maree-a. Ay too?)
My name is Mary. And yours?

Dove stai?
(Dovay stah-ee?)
Where are you staying?

Sto laggiù.
(Stoh lajjoo.)
I'm staying over there.

Quanti anni hai?
(Kwantee anee eye?)
How old are you?

Ho sette anni.
(O settay annee.)
I am seven.

No
(No)
No

Grazie
(Grazee-ay)
Thank you

Arrivederci
(Arree-vedair-chee)
Goodbye

Buona sera
(Bwona sayra)
Good evening

Mi dispiace
(Mee deespee-achay)
I'm sorry

Signora
(Seenyora)
Mrs, Madam

Signorina
(Seenyoreena)
Miss

27

At the café

un'insalata mista
(oon'eensalarta meesta)
a mixed salad

una pizza
(oona peezah)
a pizza

il menù
(eel maynoo)
the menu

Here are some people ordering food and drink at a café. They are using the word Vorrei, which means I would like. Using this word you can order any of the items around the picture.

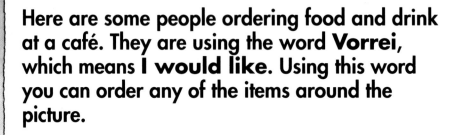

Che cosa desiderano?
(Kay koza dayseed-ayrano?)
What would you like?

Vorrei un panino con prosciutto e una Coca-Cola.
(Vorray oon paneeno con proshootto ay oona Coca-Cola.)
I would like a ham roll and a Coca-Cola.

un bicchiere
(oon beekee-airay)
a glass

un pasticcino
(oon pasticheeno)
a little cake

il cameriere
(eel kamairee-airay)
waiter

un gelato alla fragola
(oon jelarto alla fragola)
a strawberry ice-cream

una bottiglia d'acqua
(oona botteel-ya d'akwa)
a bottle of water

una brioche
(oona breeosh)
a sweet roll

un panino con salame
(oon paneeno con salarmay)
a roll with salami

Quale gusto – fragola, cioccolato o crema?
(Kwalay goosto – fragola, chockolato o krayma?)
Which flavour – strawberry, chocolate or vanilla?.

Vorrei un gelato.
(Vorray oon jelarto.)
I would like an ice-cream.

Cameriere! Il conto, per favore.
(Kamairee-airay! Eel konto, pair favoray.)
Waiter! The bill please.

la pasta
(la pasta)
pasta

il conto
(eel konto)
the bill

l'olio e l'aceto
(l'oleeo ay l'achayto)
oil and vinegar

la cameriera
(la kamairee-aira)
waitress

il sale e il pepe
(eel salay ay eel paypay)
salt and pepper

delle patate fritte
(dayl-lay patartay frittay)
some chips

At the shops

la marmellata
(la marmayllarta)
jam

le caramelle
(lay kara-mellay)
sweets

le olive
(lay o-leevay)
olives

le uova
(lay wova)
eggs

il latte
(eel lattay)
milk

il pane
(eel panay)
bread

le pesche
(lay payskay)
peaches

i biscotti
(ee biscottee)
biscuits

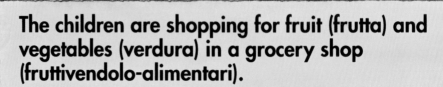

The children are shopping for fruit (frutta) and vegetables (verdura) in a grocery shop (fruttivendolo-alimentari).

Desidera?
(Dayseed-ayra?)
What would you like?

Vorrei un chilo di mele per favore.
(Vorray oon keelo dee maylay pair favoray.)
I would like a kilo of apples please.

il pollo
(eel pollo)
chicken

il giornale
(eel jornarlay)
newspaper

la torta
(la torta)
cake

le zucchine
(lay zoockeenay)
courgettes

il salame
(eel salarmay)
salami

Around the pictures are some useful words for things you might want to buy in other shops using the same word Vorrei.

il fumetto
(eel foomaytto)
comic

Quante ne vuole?
(Kwantay nay vwolay?)
How many would you like?

Due lattughe per favore.
(Doo-ay lattoogay pair favoray.)
Two lettuces please.

le melanzane
(lay melanzanee)
aubergines

il formaggio
(eel formajo)
cheese

i francobolli
(ee franko-bollee)
stamps

il pesce
(eel payshay)
fish

i pomodori
(ee pomodoree)
tomatoes

la crema per il sole
(la krayma pair eel solay)
suntan cream

Index

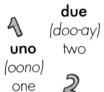

1 **uno** *(oono)* one

2 **due** *(doo-ay)* two

3 **tre** *(tray)* three

4 **quattro** *(kwattro)* four

5 **cinque** *(cheenkway)* five

6 **sei** *(say)* six

7 **sette** *(sayttay)* seven

8 **otto** *(otto)* eight

9 **nove** *(novay)* nine

10 **dieci** *(dee-aychee)* ten

gennaio *(jen-eye-yo)* January

nero *(nayro)* black

bianco *(bee-anko)* white

rosso *(rosso)* red

arancio *(arancho)* orange

verde *(vairday)* green

blu *(blu)* blue

lunedì *(loonaydee)* Monday

martedì *(martaydee)* Tuesday

Alps 8
Apulia 9
Arco di Constantino 11
Basilica di San Pietro 11
Buonarroti, Michelangelo 21
Capri 23
Colosseo 11
Columbus, Christopher 21
Courmayeur 22
Da Vinci, Leonardo 21
Drink 14-15, 28-29
European Economic
 Community 21
Farming 17
Festivals 24-25
Fishing 17
Flag, of Italy 6
Florence 22
Fontana di Trevi 11
Food 14-15, 28-29
Galileo Galilei 21
Garibaldi, Giuseppe 20
History, of Italy 20-21
Industry 16
Isola Bella 23
Italy, map of 4-5
Lake Maggiore 23
Language 6, 26-31
Latium 9
Leaning Tower of Pisa 23
Money 7
Mont Blanc 4

Monumento a Vittorio
 Emanuele 11
Mount Etna 5
Mount Vesuvius 23
Mussolini, Benito 21
Naples 25
Pantheon 11
Pianura Padana 9
Piazza di Spagna &
 Spanish Steps 11
Po, River 4
Polo, Marco 21
Pompeii 23
Ponte Vecchio 22
Population 6
Produce 8, 16-17
Roman Forum 10
Rome 10-11
Sardinia 4
School 18-19
Shops 12-13, 30-31
Sicily 5, 23
Siena 24
Sport 19
St Mark's Square 22
Tourism 16
Tuscany 9
Umbria 9
Venice 22,24
Victor Emmanuel 20
Vivaldi, Antonio 21
Weather 8

febbraio *(febr-eye-yo)* February

marzo *(martso)* March

aprile *(apreelay)* April

maggio *(majo)* May

giugno *(joonyo)* June

luglio *(loolyo)* July

agosto *(agosto)* August

settembre *(settembray)* September

ottobre *(ottobray)* October

novembre *(novembray)* November

mercoledì *(maircolaydee)* Wednesday

giovedì *(jovaydee)* Thursday

venerdì *(vaynairdee)* Friday

sabato *(sabato)* Saturday

domenica *(domayneeka)* Sunday

dicembre *(deechembray)* December

how my body works

sleeping

Mike Reid

Wayland

how my body works

Breathing
Eating
Growing
Moving
Sleeping
Staying Healthy

Editor: Anna Girling
Designer: Jean Wheeler

First published in 1992 by
Wayland (Publishers) Ltd
61 Western Road, Hove
East Sussex BN3 1JD, England

British Library Cataloguing in Publication Data
Reid, Mike
Sleeping.—(How my body works)
I. Title   II. Series
612.821

ISBN 0 7502 0406 0

Typeset by Dorchester Typesetting Group Ltd
Printed and bound in Belgium by Casterman S.A.

All words printed in **bold** are explained in the glossary.

Contents

Why do I need to sleep?   4

What happens when I do not sleep?   6

How long do I sleep?   8

What happens to my body when I sleep?   10

What do I do at bedtime?   12

How do I get to sleep?   14

What do we sleep in?   16

What is a snore?   18

What do I dream about?   20

How else can I rest my body?   22

Does everyone sleep at night?   24

Do animals sleep?   26

Where do animals sleep?   28

Glossary   30

Books to read   30

Notes on the National Curriculum   31

Index   32

Why do I need to sleep?

You need to sleep to give your body a rest. Think of all the things you have done today.

You cannot do all this every day without sleeping. Your body would get too tired.

When you wake up after a good sleep you feel ready to start again. Do you stretch when you wake up?

What happens when I do not sleep?

Have you ever stayed up late? How did you feel the next day?

If you do not have enough sleep you may find that you do things more slowly. You may find it hard to **concentrate**. You may even be grumpy.

6

What time is your bedtime? Even if you go to bed early you may not go to sleep straight away. What stops you from sleeping?

A baby crying

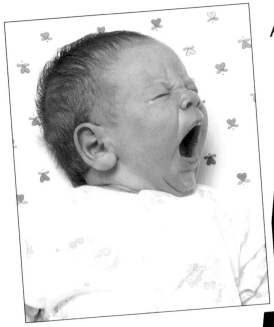

The wind in the trees

A dog barking

7

If you go to sleep at 8 o'clock at night, and wake up at 8 o'clock in the morning, you will have been asleep for twelve hours. What time do you usually go to sleep at night?

8

Find out how many hours you slept last night. Find out how many hours your friends and family slept. Make a chart of your findings like this one.

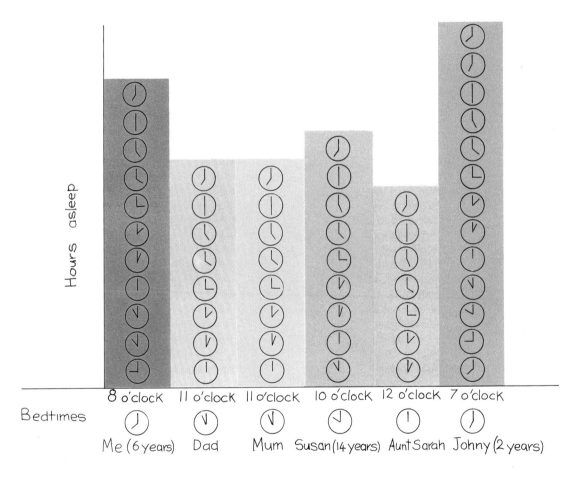

Who spent the most time asleep? How many hours did they sleep?

What happens to my body when I sleep?

Have you ever watched anyone sleeping? What did you notice?

People **breathe** even when they are asleep. They have their eyes closed. They still move about. Some people even walk in their sleep.

Other things happen while you sleep but you cannot see them. Your heart is beating slowly. Your food is being **digested**. Your body is being kept warm.

What do I do at bedtime?

What do you do at bedtime before you go to sleep? These pictures show some of the things you may do.

You clean your teeth.

You have a wash.

You put
on your
pyjamas.

You read a bedtime story. You have a
bedtime drink. You go to the toilet.
What order would you do these things in?
Do you do anything else?

When you go to bed you may go straight to sleep. Some children find this difficult. They may worry about shadows in the dark. They may hear strange noises. They **imagine** all sorts of things, but there really is no need to worry.

There are lots of things that can help you get to sleep. You may like to cuddle a **favourite** toy. You may like a bedtime story. You may like a light left on.

What do we sleep in?

Who would sleep in
these beds?

A cot

A hammock

A bunk bed

A sleeping-bag

Which ones have you slept in?

When you are asleep you are still breathing. Air comes into your body through your nose and mouth. Sometimes when you breathe through your mouth you make a noise. This noise is called a snore.

18

What is a yawn?

A yawn just happens. A yawn is when you open your mouth wide and take in a deep breath. You yawn when you are sleepy.

What do I dream about?

Every night when we are asleep we have
dreams. When we wake up we have usually
forgotten them. Can you remember any of your
dreams?

Bad dreams are called nightmares.
Sometimes they wake us up.

How else can I rest my body?

If you have been rushing around, you use up a lot of **energy**. You get tired. You may need to give your body a short rest.

You do not have to go to sleep. There are other ways of resting. Look at these pictures. What are these children doing?

Chatting

Watching television

22

Playing a game

Reading a book

23

Does everyone sleep at night?

When you are sleeping, some people are awake. They have to work through the night to get things ready for the next day.

This man is sorting letters ready to be delivered in the morning.

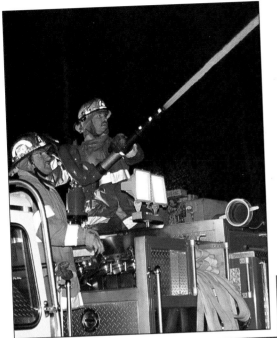

Some people stay awake at night in case someone needs their help.

Who would help if there was a fire?

Who would help if you were ill?

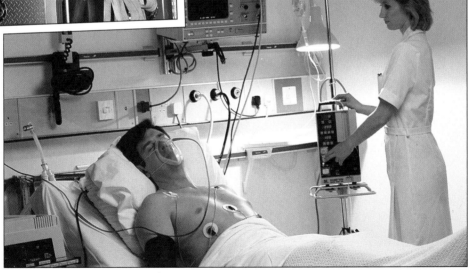

People who work at night go to sleep during the day.

Do animals sleep?

Like us, all animals need to sleep. Some sleep at night and are awake during the day. Dogs sleep at night.

Some animals sleep during the day and are awake at night. These animals are called 'nocturnal'. An owl is nocturnal.

Some animals sleep for a very long time. They sleep all through the winter. We say that they 'hibernate'. They wake up in the spring when the weather is warmer. A dormouse hibernates.

Where do animals sleep?

Look at these drawings of animals and the places where they sleep. Try to match them up. The first one has been done for you.

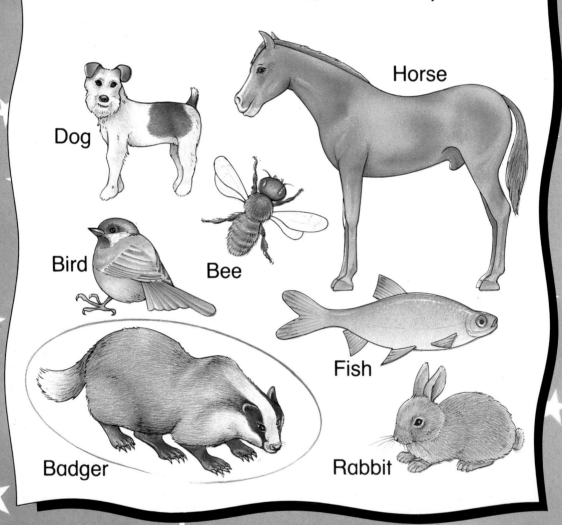

Dog

Horse

Bird

Bee

Fish

Badger

Rabbit

Hive

Pond

Set

Stable

Kennel

Tree

Burrow

Answers on page 32

Glossary

Breathe To take air in and out of your lungs.
Concentrate To keep your mind on what you are doing.
Digest To break down food in your stomach so that your body can use it.

Energy The ability and strength to move and do things.
Favourite The thing you like best.
Imagine To picture something to yourself in your mind.

Books to read

Bad Mood Bear by John Richardson (Arrow, 1990)
In My Bedroom by Carol Thompson (Walker, 1991)
Let's Talk About After Dark by Maria Marinez i Vendrell (Magi, 1989)
Nandy's Bedtime by Errol Lloyd (Random Century, 1991)
What a Noise! by Neil Morris (Firefly, 1990)

There are many stories about sleeping that you can read. Try to find these stories: *Rip Van Winkle*; *Goldilocks and the Three Bears*; *Sleeping Beauty*.